Table of Contents

INTRODUCTION

A BRIEF HISTORY

CATS IN PUBLIC SERVICE

THE MOST FAMOUS CAT LOVERS

HOW CATS DEFEATED NAPOLEON

MISCONCEPTIONS OF CATS' INTELLECT

A CAT'S REASONING, CONSCIOUSNESS, AND SELF-AWARENESS

A CAT'S INTELLIGENCE

WHAT SCIENTISTS HAVE TO SAY

HOW CATS THINK

HOW CATS LEARN

THE TRIAL AND ERROR METHOD

CAT'S THINK DIFFERENTLY

WHO IS MANIPULATING WHOM?

THREE MYTHS ABOUT THE INTELLIGENCE OF CATS

10 CAT SECRETS

5 LIFEHACKS FOR OWNERS

HOW TO NEGOTIATE WITH YOUR CAT

HOW CATS COMMUNICATE WITH PEOPLE

WHAT DOES RUBBING AGAINST AN OWNER MEAN IN CAT LANGUAGE?

THE SIGNALS OF YOUR CAT'S TAIL

READING YOUR CAT'S EYES

THE POSITION OF YOUR CAT'S EARS

THE SIGNALS OF YOUR CAT'S WHISKERS

YOUR CAT'S PAW SIGNALS

WHAT YOUR CAT'S POSTURE IS SAYING

WHY DOES MY CAT LICK ITS COAT?

THE LANGUAGE OF PURRING

- [WHY DOES MY CAT SCREAM?](#)
- [THE MEANING OF "MEOW"](#)
- [COMMUNICATION OF CATS AMONGST THEMSELVES](#)
- [CULTIVATING MUTUAL UNDERSTANDING BETWEEN YOU AND YOUR CAT](#)
- [RESPECTING YOUR CAT](#)
- [COMFORTABLE LIVING CONDITIONS](#)
- [ADMONISHING YOUR CAT](#)
- [SOLICITING FRIENDSHIP BETWEEN PETS](#)
- [STRENGTHENING YOUR RELATIONSHIP WITH YOUR PET](#)
- [MY CAT IS AN ALIEN](#)
- [CONCLUSION](#)

INTRODUCTION

Sometimes I look into my cat's eyes and try to figure out what she's thinking. I want to speak to her and tell her about myself. I see that she listens to me. I think she understands me. When I'm sad, she comes to lie down next to me and purrs. When I'm in pain, she finds the sore spot, lies down, and relieves the pain.

She makes me feel better. Sometimes she walks up, looks me in the eye, and starts meowing. I understand that she's asking for something. I know my cat, and, more often than not, I can guess her mood and desires by her habits and behavior. There is a mutual understanding between us; we are happy.

This book is for cat lovers. It will help you recognize the thoughts, desires, behaviors, and moods of your pet in order to foster mutual understanding and love between you.

A BRIEF HISTORY

Did you know that the ancient ancestors of our felines are as old as dinosaurs, little creatures living in the forest millions of years ago? While larger dinosaurs became extinct due to lack of food, these smaller creatures survived, and, through the centuries, came into our homes as the cats we know and love today.

Even in ancient Egypt, cats were revered as sacred animals because they guarded grain storehouses against rodents. Cats have also always found homes on ships and submarines But what good is a cat on a sub? Living in constant confinement, far from home, crewmates need a psychological release, and a cat is an excellent living "antidepressant."

Just petting the animals can have a beneficial effect on the health of the sailors — blood pressure may be lowered, morale improves. Furthermore, a cat's sensitive nose works much better than any gas monitor and can instantly detect an increase in concentrations of harmful gases in a submarine's compartments.

CATS IN PUBLIC SERVICE

In the United Kingdom, the Royal Navy has maintained a guild of ship cats for several centuries. Each furry sailor has laissez-passer and may serve on any of the ships of Her Majesty's fleet. The tradition continues to this day.

Cats serve in the UK Prime Minister's residence, the foreign ministry, the Ministry of Finance, and in museums, including the famous Russian Hermitage and Winter Palace. Cats live in the palace itself and come to work every day. They are paid a salary in meat. Each feline has its own passport complete with a photo, just like people. And in Japan, a cat even works as a railway stationmaster.

Cats can predict earthquakes. They detect positive ions in the air, which are released in huge numbers during the build-up of an earthquake.

Another interesting fact: during World War II, cats often sensed an imminent bombing and warned their owners. Europeans, in thanks to their furry friends, established a special award for animal bravery engraved with the words "We also serve."

THE MOST FAMOUS CAT LOVERS

Cats were loved by the monarchs of Europe (Queen Victoria of Great Britain) and heads of state (British PM Winston Churchill), not to mention Sister of Mercy and British public figure Florence Nightengale, who kept sixty cats, or the writer Mark Twain, who had nineteen cats. The great physicist Isaac Newton is credited with inventing the pet door.

HOW CATS DEFEATED NAPOLEON

Among these great people, however, are those who didn't like cats. They include Napoleon Bonaparte, Alexander the Great, Genghis Khan, and Caesar. The famous English Admiral Nelson knew that Napoleon was afraid of cats and, ahead of battle with the approaching French army, released about seventy cats onto the battlefield. Napoleon was frightened greatly, demoralized, and lost the battle.

MISCONCEPTIONS OF CATS' INTELLECT

Many mistakenly believe that cats are not smart enough to be trained. It is also known that cats become attached not to people, but their homes. That said, every cat has its own character, and its behavior can often surprise and confuse an owner. There are endless stories of cats' characters and behaviors, but what is true? What are our cats really thinking? What do they like and dislike? How can we understand their language and desires?

Cats do not think abstractly and have no idea of the concept of the past and future. Here, some might be offended and try to prove that I am underestimating our feline friends, that they are more than base reflexes.

The absence of abstract thinking does not mean that a cat instantly forgets any given event that has just occurred. It will remember the event, but only when some meaningful stimulus reminds it.

You should not consider your cat's experience to be a series of past events that it remembers. Rather, you must consider what is happening in the present. But sometimes, a conditioned stimulus, an event that has been clearly imprinted in your cat's brain, will link it to the past.

For example, if a cat is bitten by a dog, the stimuli that will link the cat to these traumatic memories are the smell of the dog and/or its barking, appearance, etc. It just so happens that these stimuli are so powerful that a feline will remember the attacker and begin to fear, or sometimes, on the contrary, show aggression to animals of a certain color or breed, or a person of a certain sex.

But if this "link" in the form of a conditioned stimulus is not present at any given moment, a cat is simply not thinking of the event. Our cats do not sit in an armchair by the fireplace on a cold evening, indulging sad memories of some tragic event that happened five years ago. Only we do that.

The future is a different question entirely. Cats are unable to imagine that which hasn't happened yet. They cannot dream. That is, they cannot imagine something that doesn't exist. Consequently, the biggest problem of adapting a cat is preparing it for upcoming events. There is no way to do this; they are not aware of the future. They live strictly in the present.

For this reason, any move, change of family composition, change of food, rearrangement in the home, or a trip to the vet can be stressful for our felines. Humans can prepare themselves and their nervous systems for a frightening event.

For example, we can adjust to a trip to the dentist or gradually come to decisions about changing jobs or residences. Cats are unable to do this because, to them, the future does not exist.

However! Cats can intuit how to behave after awhile in order to avoid trouble, but, once again, they are guided by stimuli. For example, an owner takes the cat carrier out of the closet, turns around, and his cat is nowhere to be found. By itself, the carrier isn't a threat, but a conditioned response, the fear of a trip to the vet, can be very powerful for a cat.

Traveling in the carrier becomes a kind of hyperlink to this specific fear. Upon seeing the crate, the animal begins to feel the same fear and tries to hide. Some animals learn to detect these stimuli so subtly that their hosts begin to suspect them of being telepaths.

But cats have only the here and now, plus some intelligence and associative thinking — a kind of flashback that pops up in the brain in response to positive and negative stimuli. This is why any changes in a cat's life are to it what sudden natural disasters are to us. If you still don't understand what exactly the absence of abstract thinking means, remember that toddlers also lack this ability. First, try to remember the events of your adulthood. How you passed this or that exam, or your thesis topic, for example. Can you remember them?

Now, try to recall yourself at one or two years old. Do you remember everything clearly? How you were potty trained, how your diapers were changed, how you learned to walk and talk. Personally, I remember nothing from this time; my first memories are from the ages of four or five.

All that being said, a one- or two-year-old child is not a robot, they run, play, love their mothers, feel pain, know how to get attention, laugh and cry, recognize loved ones, and might even make some meaningful observations. However, like cats, toddlers do not have abstract thinking abilities. Unlike cats, on the other hand, these abilities quickly develop as the child grows.

A CAT'S REASONING, CONSCIOUSNESS, AND SELF-AWARENESS

So, do cats have the ability to reason? Of course, they can't "reason" or "think" as we, as humans, may define the word. However, they can process the information coming to their brains. It is upon this information that they base their next actions.

Felines have internal ideas about the world around them. Cats can understand certain physical laws like object permanence (objects do not cease to exist when they are invisible to the eye). They have an innate sense of time, they can identify other cats, some people, and a number of objects.

People have created the definition of intelligence, and, as such, they judge intelligence as it exists on the human scale. Children are taught to look where a finger points. A cat, however, will look to the pointing finger itself instead. In order to bring the cat's attention to an object, you need to touch the object itself.

A CAT'S INTELLIGENCE

One of the parameters of intellectual development is self-awareness.

A popular test of self-awareness is to observe how a subject (human or animal) reacts to its reflection in a mirror.

Humans and higher primates recognize their reflections. If you smear some paint on a child's or chimpanzee's nose and let them look at themselves in the mirror, they will try to wipe the paint from their face, not from the reflection.

If a mirror is placed in front of a cat, it will first look for the unfamiliar animal hiding behind the mirror. Then the cat will realize that the cat in the mirror isn't real and will ignore it (this ability to ignore the reflection is necessary, or a cat would not be able to drink water, seeing its reflection in it). Unlike humans and higher primates, a cat does not understand that the reflection in the mirror is itself.

Cat behavior researcher Secha Schofield has a different opinion of the definition of self-awareness in cats. In fact, she suggests that the mirror test isn't applicable to cats at all. It does not give an objective assessment of the way non-social subjects, namely cats, think.

She hypothesizes that the cat loses interest in its reflection in the mirror because it perceives it as another cat that has no interest in interacting. Schofield believes that the cat views the image in the mirror as a reflection of the real world and uses it to observe objects that are out of sight.

The researcher observed how her own cats sometimes looked at each other at her through the mirror. There were times when her cats, upon seeing her reflection in the mirror, began to meow in greeting, suggesting that they recognized the reflection of their owner in the mirror.

Moving into a new home, one of her cats, fifteen-year-old Flossie, often used a mirror to watch family members. She looked through the mirror from the hallway into the bedroom, and vice versa. It's possible that she used the mirror to compensate for her deafness, that is, it may have been convenient for Flossie to use the mirror to determine whether another cat was approaching from behind.

To determine whether the cat understands the mirror correctly, it is placed in front of the mirror while the researcher stands behind. The researcher then makes gestures and notes whether the cat responds to the reflection or turns and reacts to the person directly. It should be noted, however, that the cat could also be responding to other stimuli, like a sound, from the person behind them.

Schofield believes that a cat is not interested in its own reflection because it doesn't care about its own appearance. Subjects that recognize themselves in their reflections are social creatures — humans, monkeys, and parrots, for example. Much depends on their physical attractiveness, as perceived by other members of the species. People who have little interest in attracting attention to themselves or in their social position are usually uninterested in their appearance.

In the hierarchy of cats, most important is good health and physical endurance. An attractive appearance, on the other hand, has no place at all. Unlike species that perceive their own kind through their sense of sight, cats understand the world around them through a mixture of senses — smells, sounds, sights, and touch (using their whiskers). There are better equipped to observe a moving object than a stationary one.

Some researchers believe that even if a cat recognizes itself in a mirror, it has no motivation to react to its reflection in any way because it isn't a social animal.

If classical science states that a cat has no self-awareness, it doesn't mean that it also has no intelligence. A cat's intelligence applies to its ecological niche and is limited by physical abilities and innate behavior, or instinct.

Instincts are programmed by the brain to help a creature survive and to free up the regions of the brain dedicated to the process of thinking. Over the course of its life, your cat hones its instincts and learns things evolution could never have seen coming — opening doors, mastering tricks and commands (if an owner has the patience and time), recognizing the sound of your car's engine, and waking you up at the same time every morning.

Cats are sweet, gentle, and affectionate animals that bless many of our homes. Our pets help us relieve stress, have healing abilities, and, simply, bring diversity to our lives.

Cats are also quite intelligent creatures. However, few can understand what their favorite pets are thinking. Therefore, we need to tackle the question of how to understand what our cats think. Cats think of humans as big cats.

Cats may perceive people as big cats. They perceive their owners as a mother or father who takes care of them from birth. Therefore, to a cat, its owner is a big, naked feline that indulges their whims and cares and cherishes for them.

WHAT SCIENTISTS HAVE TO SAY

According to scientists, cats are quite intelligent animals. It is very difficult for a predator, like cats, to survive in the wild without thinking through each of their steps. Moreover, our pets have complex instincts that are the precursors of reason. But often an owner can't understand his pet's thoughts or doesn't understand that a cat is able to think in the first place.

HOW CATS THINK

Why does my cat sleep so much? Is this normal? Can cats think? These questions interest many loving owners. Cats are more than just playful, purring creatures. They can understand many aspects of human life and often manipulate people by learning simple rules. Children and animals are the best manipulators.

To understand how cats think, one needs to understand how quickly our pets learn our actions and mannerisms. For example, a cat will begin to learn what actions precede its owner's trip to the store. In response, the feline might wait for the return of the breadwinner, and hopefully some delicious food, from the store.

There are often cases when an owner specifically shows their cat what they've purchased, offering a look into the bag. Cats will remember this ritual. The next time the owner picks up the same bag, the cat already knows that he is going to the store for food for him. How could one believe cats are unthinking creatures after such an experience?

Why does my cat purr?

The purring of cats is truly captivating. It's soothing. But what exactly does the purring of our pets mean, and how do they do it? Let's consider the questions in more detail.

Today, it is not known for certain how cats reproduce such sounds. Some biologists claim that purring is achieved through the contraction of muscles that are connected to the hyoid bones, which are located near the vocal cords. The vibration of the larynx can cause the hyoid bone to resonate, making the sound we know as purring.

Often, purring is caused by a signal of muscle contraction in the brain, for example, when stroking a cat. Accordingly, he is satisfied and thanks his master for his affection with his purring.

Cats may purr in communication with one another, as a way of saying that there's no reason for any alarm or excitement as they sense no danger or aggression.

They may also purr to relax themselves after a stressful or frightening experience. You can hear the pleasant rumbling when the cat thanks its owner for a tasty meal.

Cats may also purr when a person pets them because cats undoubtedly like it. Their purring is a sign of their pleasure at the show of attention from their owner.

How to learn from a cat's tail and face. If one wants to truly understand their favorite fluffy feline, they need to first observe the pet's habits. Cats show their moods in a variety of ways, but not all owners understand what their pet wants at the moment.

So, what is your cat's tail telling you? Experts say that a cat's dissatisfaction with seeing an unfamiliar or unpleasant person can be expressed with a raised, trembling tail.

When kittens are present, a mother cat's raised tail may indicate that she is afraid for her offspring. When a cat holds its tail straight up with a bent tip, almost like a question mark, it means the cat is thinking. Though the pet may be in a good and cheerful mood, its mind is busy with its own affairs, and it wants to be left to its thoughts.

Abused cats, subjected to violence and constant shouting from their owners, express their fear in the form of an arched back and a tucked tail.

Sometimes a cat shows its fear with a fluffy tail. If its bottom is lowered down, then the cat is sad. If it twitches its tail, it means that the cat is uncomfortable with something unusual or unfamiliar happening around it. A twitching tail, for example, may accompany the move to a new home.

When an owner begins preparing for a move, gathering things together in boxes, the cat does not understand what is happening, why they can not stay in the same place. If the cat begins to beat its tail, shake, and meow nervously, it means that someone or something is causing them to be afraid.

Cats also have excellent eyesight and can see things that people cannot at first glance. Remember, when all family members love their fluffy pet, its tail is always raised in happiness and can often sway leisurely from side to side.

A cat's facial expressions. Determining a cat's mood by its face is a more difficult task. However, when we take a scientific approach, such a thing is feasible.

Pay special attention to your cat's eyes. They can speak much more eloquently than words. An aggressive cat stares at point-blank range, without looking away, its pupils are narrowed. The whiskers stick out, and the ears are pressed flat against the head.

When a cat is ready to attack, it opens its mouth, baring its teeth and gums. When cats are scared, their pupils dilate until they are almost the size of the entire eye. When at rest, the pupils narrow and the eyes close slightly.

A cat's ears can also indicate its current mood. If a cat's ears are pressed flat to its head, it may be a warning of its bad mood. If the ears are held back, the animal is afraid of something. If the cat moves its ears in all directions, it may mean that it is interested in something.

A cat with an arched back, stretched out paws, and a tail standing straight like a pipe is warning a potential enemy not to approach. The cat is ready to attack. The same bodily expressions can be observed when a cat sees itself in a mirror.

When a cat approaches and rubs against its owner's legs, it needs something. It may be hungry or want some affection, for example.

Cats express their thoughts, desires, and moods through their bodies. Learning how to read your cat's body will foster more understanding between you and your feline friend.

Any behavioral problems of your pet can be solved if you understand how cats think — why they act in one way as opposed to another. To many owners, the behavior of their pet seems mysterious and unpredictable. In fact, everything is much simpler and more complex at the same time — as always happens when the human factor is added to the equation.

HOW CATS LEARN

Cats, like all other animals, have innate and acquired skills and behaviors. Innate skills come in the form of instincts, while acquired skills are learned throughout a cat's life based on its unique experiences. If an action leads to a positive result, the animal will try to repeat said action — a form of positive reinforcement. Negative reinforcement, however, can also influence the behavior of your pet.

For example, if at one time a cat jumped up into its owner's lap, and they showered it with pets and kisses, then it will most likely climb back into their arms again and again. If the owner rudely threw the cat to the floor, however, it is unlikely the animal will seek affection from its owner again.

Remember, all animals may behave strangely and unpredictably, regardless of how well an owner feels they understand their pet's innate and acquired skills and behaviors. For example, often owners notice that a cat suffering from a urinary tract infection will stop using its litter box.

The reason for this is that when a cat experiences pain when urinating, they associate the pain with their litter box, so they look for "painless" places to relieve themselves. As the animal recovers and the pain gradually passes, the cat will sooner or later find a place where they will not experience pain.

They will then associate this new spot as a safe and painless place to do their business, all while puzzled and frustrated owners wonder why they can't get their animal to return to the litter box.

THE TRIAL AND ERROR METHOD

American scientist Edward Thorndike, through his experiments, discovered how cats think, or rather, what method of training is the most effective for them.

Thorndike put a cat in a cage that could only be opened by pulling a rope loop. Outside, he placed a piece of fish and watched as the cat tried to get out of the cage to get its treat.

It turned out that Thorndike's cats were unable to copy the actions of other cats who had learned how to open the cage. The demonstration did not help them in any way. When the scientist took a cat's paw in his hands and pulled the rope loop, the door opened. But the cat did not realize the connection between the action and the cage opening.

All cats, without exception, performed the same actions when they were first placed in the cage. They tried to squeeze through all the bars, scratched at the floor of the cage, bit the bars with their teeth and pulled with their claws, reached their paws between them, trying to reach the fish, etc.

Eventually, sooner or later, the cats accidentally got a paw into the rope loop and opened the door. Naturally, the association was still a little weak after just one repetition, but with some repeated success, the cats began to go straight to the rope.

This is how the trial and error method works, and this is how cats learn and interact with the world around them.

CAT'S THINK DIFFERENTLY

Cats have better memory than dogs. Thanks to this, they always return home from long journeys. They can usually remember the consequences of an action, good or bad, so that they can try to repeat or avoid it, to their benefit.

In doing so, our cats also begin to train us. If you wake up at five in the morning to feed your animal, it will wake you up at the same time every day, repeating and reinforcing the actions that have already proven successful.

WHO IS MANIPULATING WHOM?

People assume cats think like they do, choosing the most correct and effective action to get their way. In fact, as numerous experiments by Thorndike and other scientists prove, not only with cats but dogs as well, our pets don't actually comprehend the logic behind a successful action, the action simply becomes fixed in their behavior through positive or negative reinforcement.

Animals do not comprehend a situation as we do. They do not follow the logic between an action and its result. This is easy to prove; changing the conditions of Thorndike's cage experiment. For example, move the door to the other side of the cage, and the cat will look for it again, completely forgetting that they've already solved the puzzle.

So it's not cats that manipulate us, necessarily, but we that manipulate ourselves with cats! Simply change the "conditions of the experiment" — do not get up at five in the morning to feed your pet, move the "painful" litter box to another place, or buy another one. Your task is to turn the situation around so that the result is favorable for both you and your feline.

THREE MYTHS ABOUT THE INTELLIGENCE OF CATS

Cats are extremely intelligent creatures. Ethologists (scientists who study the behavior of animals) have long established that they can not only maintain causal relationships, think abstractly, solve complex multi-pass problems, and count, but even intentionally deceive a person!

The habits and peculiarities of our cats have long aroused interest. And the inherent mystery of these animals has given rise to a huge number of myths and prejudices, some of which we will try to debunk today.

MYTH #1

Cats are not very smart — they are not adaptable to education or training.

Cats are naturally curious creatures. They are attracted to anything new, unusual, or bright. If you take advantage of this aspect of your cat's personality, then training your animal in simple household skills and more complex tasks can become much easier.

Furthermore, the consequence of a cat's intellect is sometimes stubbornness. The cat perfectly understands what the owner wants from it, but repetitions of the same tasks only irritate it.

It is useless to beat and punish the cat. It will only become angry and stop responding entirely to the owner's attempts to teach it.

MYTH #2

Meowing is the language of communication between cats.

Cats' high level of intelligence and social motivation has allowed them to develop a special language for communicating with their owners. Yes, this is the "meow" - used only with us! Cats don't meow among themselves. Recent research by zoopsychologists at Cornell University has proven that cats are perfectly capable of expressing themselves and their desires to their owners.

MYTH #3

Cats are very cunning — they behave badly to spite their owners.

In fact, behavioral problems most often occur in cats that are under stress. Cats do not tolerate radical changes in their surroundings well, be it moving, renovations, or the appearance of a new person in the house. If the cat has become unbearable, it may be sick or depressed.

Cats are very sensitive to changes in the psychological climate of the house. Regular family scandals and quarrels can lead to serious diseases and a decline in mental health and intelligence in cats.

10 CAT SECRETS

1. Only domestic cats hold their tail straight up in the air. In the wild, the feline tail either hangs near the ground or is raised no higher than the back. Perhaps big cats are just trying to be inconspicuous. If the animal starts hunting, then the protruding tail can easily give away the predator.

2. It is believed that cats are unable to taste sweetness. Scientists say that, despite the presence of receptors for sweetness, cats, all the same, cannot taste it. This is explained by a mutation of the T1R2 gene, which occurred due to the carnivorous diet of most cats.

Many owners are quick to challenge this statement, saying that their animals love condensed milk, whipped cream, or ice cream. Most likely, these products are appreciated by cats not for their sweetness, but for the presence of milk in them.

3. It is known that cats, despite having a lower social IQ than dogs, outperform them in solving complex cognitive tasks. The necessary condition — the cat's interest.

4. People love purring. Some experts claim that these vibrations are therapeutic for humans. But purring isn't always a sign of pleasure. It may be a sign that they are in pain, scared, or are extremely dissatisfied with something.

5. Cats do not need vitamin C, so fruits and vegetables aren't a necessary part of their diet. Vitamin C is produced and maintained in the body of cats independently.

6. Cats can, if not read your thoughts, then accurately feel you on a level inaccessible to humans. Cat owners have seen hundreds of times how the animals mysteriously seem to know when a family member is returning home. Or how cats seem to know when a trip to the vet is on the books and will hide from their owners.

7. Cat owners have probably already noticed that their animals don't really sweat. Experts explain that cats have sweat glands only on the cheeks, lips, around the nipples, and between the pads on the paws. Therefore, an owner will usually only see their cat sweating from its paws when it's stressed.

8. The cat is one of the three species of animals in the world that step with both right legs at the same, then both left legs, rather than diagonally (stepping with the front, right paw and back, left paw, then vice-versa). In addition to cats, giraffes and camels also walk in this way. This feature helps cats walk quickly and quietly.

9. Sometimes it seems that cats do not hear when their owners try to speak to them. Actually, the animals simply don't want to listen if they aren't responsive, or are simply more interested in something else. They have excellent hearing. There are thirty muscles in cats' ears that allow them to turn in any direction and more than forty thousand nerve endings.

10. Cats respond better to a woman's voice than to a man's. Most likely, this is due to the fact that women have a higher tone of voice. It is also known that when a person speaks to a cat in a high voice, like when talking to a baby, the animal perceives the words as negative. Low tones, on the other hand, are soothing for felines.

5 LIFEHACKS FOR OWNERS

1. The cat's litter box, if it's plain sight and in the way, is a big problem. There is a way to hide the cat tray, however, eliminating the eyesore and giving your pet comfort in privacy. Remove the bottom panel from a cabinet door: if it's glass, pull out the glass, if it's wooden, you can cut out a square. Place the litter box inside the cabinet and hang small curtains from the hole.

2. If you don't want a scratching post in your room, take a rope and wrap the legs of your tables and chairs. This type of scratching post can be not only useful but also create a unique aesthetic in your home.

3. Cats like to keep track of what's happening in the house. If you notice that your pet has taken up a regular spot, sitting or lying under a chair, for

example, arrange a place for it there. You can make a nifty hammock under your feline's favorite chair with a piece of fabric and some Velcro fasteners.

4. If you need to bathe your cat, it's better to do it in the sink, rather than in the bathroom. First, it will be much easier for you to clean and hold the animal. Second, the cat will be more comfortable with the owner nearby.

5. If the cat litter doesn't sufficiently block the smell, you can take a few green tea leaves and throw them in the tray. It will neutralize the unpleasant odors.

HOW TO NEGOTIATE WITH YOUR CAT

Negotiating with your cat means understanding its gestures and language. Sometimes, our cats seem like little more than disagreeable little aliens. This is far from true, however. Carefully observe your pet's behavior. You will easily notice that, with the help of movements, gestures, and facial expressions, the cat expresses a huge range of feelings, allowing you to guess the course of its thoughts.

HOW CATS COMMUNICATE WITH PEOPLE

Cats are among the most emotional animals. They can communicate their feelings through various means:

- rubbing;

- movements of the tail;

- glances;

– their mouths (licking, licking the owner, and biting, playful or otherwise);

- posture (body movements, ears, paws);

- sound signals (purring, screaming, meowing, hissing).

These simple actions express a cat's main emotions and feelings:

- love;

- desire to communicate;

- thirst;

- hunger;

- curiosity;

- annoyance;

- anger;

- the desire to be alone;

- a request for something specific.

For comfortable and effective communication with your pet, you need to learn to understand what your cat wants to "say" at any given moment. Pay close attention to the signs your feline friend is giving you, and you'll enjoy a mutual understanding between one another.

WHAT DOES RUBBING AGAINST AN OWNER MEAN IN CAT LANGUAGE?

Cats are slaves to their instincts, and their main sources of information are smells. Through them, cats communicate with the owner and other family members.

To rid the house of extraneous scents, a cat marks the boundaries of its territory with its own scent. Since its owner, in the opinion of the cat, is inviolable property, the animal marks it with the help of sebaceous glands located on the muzzle, paws, and at the base of the tail.

These glands secrete special pheromones undetectable by the human nose. In order to mark the owner, the cat follows a special ritual:

- nuzzling after a long separation;

- walking in circles at your feet;

- sniffing, while touching the tongue and mouth to the owner.

There are a few other reasons a cat might mark its owner:

- it wants to simply say hello;

- it requires food;

- it seeks affection.

A feline's pheromones act as a kind of register and alarm system in the animal's home. Some cats, however, never rub up against their owners.

This can usually be explained by a lack of trust between the animal and owner. A special mark is awarded only to those who are not dangerous and are part of the cat's world.

THE SIGNALS OF YOUR CAT'S TAIL

A cat's mood can be determined by the position of its tail with a great degree of accuracy.

A sure sign of a happy cat is a vertically raised tail. It signifies complete trust in the owner and the expectation of affection and open communication.

You will notice an especially active tail when your pet is communicating with a person or other animal.

A raised tail with a curl at the end indicates contentment with life. Perhaps the feline is showing its position as the rightful owner of its territory.

Occasional twitching of the tail can be a sign of either excitement or stress. Please consult your veterinarian if your pet's tail is twitching and can't be explained by excitement (during play, for example).

When the fur on your pet's tail bristles, it's a sign of tension and nervousness. Felines fluff up their tails as a way of presenting themselves to be larger than they really are.

A lightly shaking tail is a sign of joy upon greeting an owner. It might also indicate that your pet is waiting for a treat.

When your cat's tail sticks straight up like a pipe and it shifts its weight to its front paws, it's a sign of defensive aggression. You should attempt to calm your pet with soft touches and affection.

If a cat's tail is straight, almost level with the spine, it is likely a sign that the animal is uneasy. Some felines hold their tail straight at a forty-five-degree angle when they are confused and don't know what to make of an unfamiliar situation.

A lowered or tucked tail can be a sign of submission, but may also indicate nervousness or sickness.

A tail that is quickly swishing back and forth is a sign of an angry and aggressive feline. A tail that is slowly swaying from side to side, however, can be a sign of a focused cat that might be ready to play.

Of course, all pets are individuals, each having their own idiosyncrasies. Carefully observe your pets and learn how they react to different situations to foster more understanding between you and your furry friends.

READING YOUR CAT'S EYES

Cats, like humans, have very expressive eyes. Sometimes, you can tell what's on your feline's mind just by looking them in the eye.

Dilated pupils are indicators of strong emotions. It may be excitement, fear, joy, or aggression. When a cat enters a new home for the first time, its pupils also dilate. It needs time to get comfortable in a new environment.

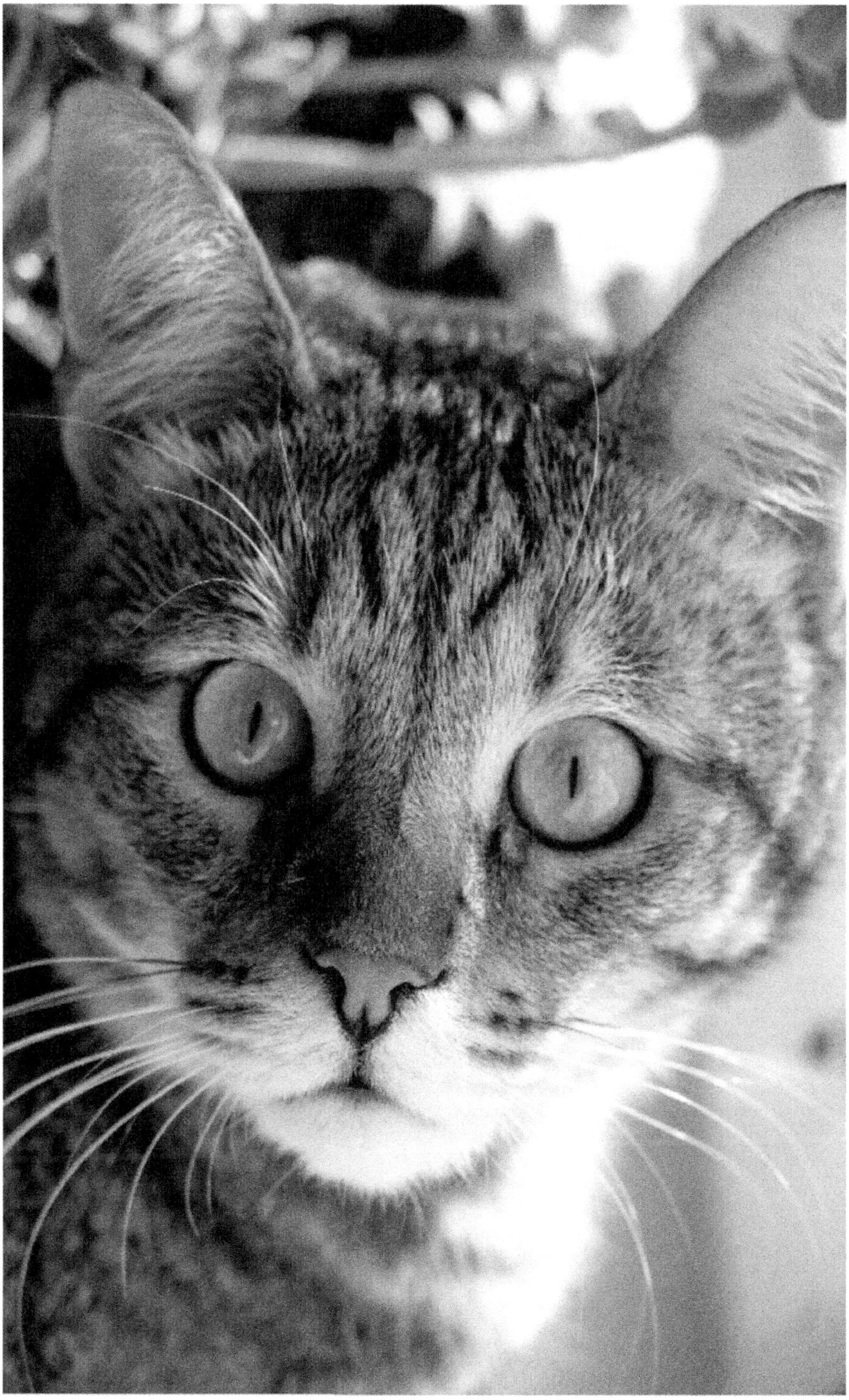

A direct gaze is a sign of trust and comfort between a cat and its owner.

Light squinting and slow blinking is a sign that a cat is well, comfortable, and calm. These eyes are often accompanied by purring.

A cat's eyes carry a lot of information, but should never be the only clue you consider when trying to understand your feline a bit better. Take advantage of all the means of communication the feline body makes use of.

THE POSITION OF YOUR CAT'S EARS

Cat's can turn their ears 180° and can move them independently of one another. They are also another good indicator of a cat's mood.

Ears raised vertically show that a cat is very interested in something.

Ears turned back and laying down flat against the head are a sure sign of fright and discomfort.

Ears pressed flat but turned slightly to the side are a sign of aggression and a cat that is ready to fight.

Erect ears that are turned back can indicate surprise or indignation.

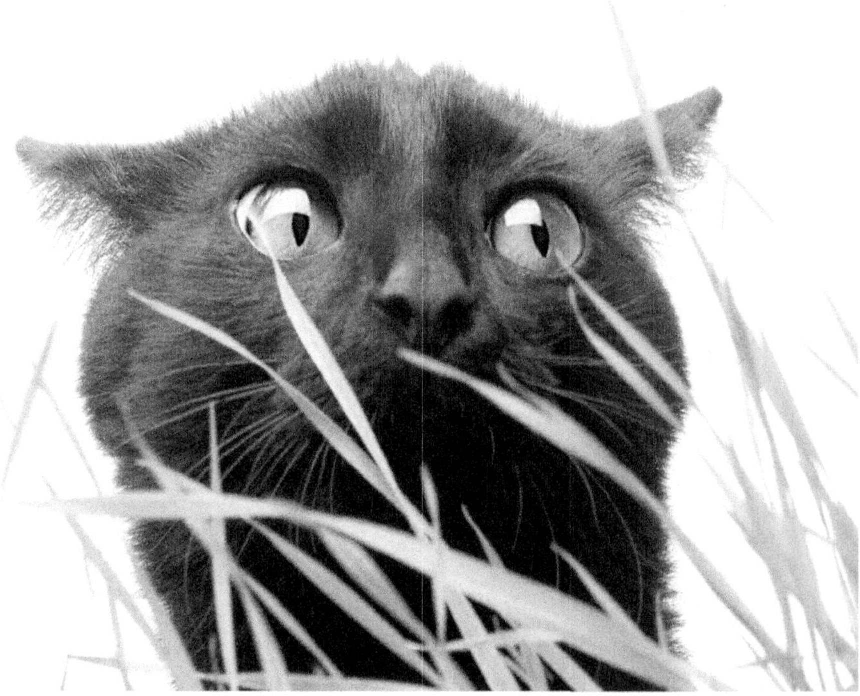

THE SIGNALS OF YOUR CAT'S WHISKERS

The next way you can more accurately read your pet's mood is its whiskers.

Whiskers pointing down signify sadness or pain.

Whiskers pointing forward are the mark of a hunter and curiosity.

Bristling whiskers are a sure sign of fright and anxiety.

Whiskers that fall loosely to the sides mean the feline is simply at rest.

YOUR CAT'S PAW SIGNALS

Our feline friends also use their paws as a main method of communication.

If a cat touches its owner with its paw, it is likely asking for something. Sometimes, to attract attention, a cat's touch is accompanied by a short purr. After making sure that it has been noticed, the animal may go on ahead, expecting the owner to follow. When the cat gently touches the owner's face with a soft paw, it's waiting for an affectionate stroke in return.

If your cat tramples you with its paws, it's expressing extreme confidence in you, at the same time marking you with its smell.

When a cat grabs its owner's hand in its paws, it's an indication of unconditional trust or a desire to play.

WHAT YOUR CAT'S POSTURE IS SAYING

Our cats use all the parts of their bodies in order to express their moods, emotions, and desires.

When your cat spins in circles around your legs, it's expressing delight and love. An accompanying headbutt is a sign of sincere affection.

A cat sitting quietly in one spot, with its tail wrapped around its body is alert, watching its territory.

A cat that offers its belly or presents its backside to you is one that trusts you to the highest degree.

Nuzzling under the arm or in the armpit of the owner is the sign of a worrying feline that seeks its owner's protection.

A cat arches its back when it's ready to fight.

If your cat turns its back to you and raises the tail vertically, it recognizes your primacy in the household.

When it rubs its whiskers against something, a cat is showing its curiosity in the object.

A cat that grooms its owner by licking them or biting their hair is simply trying to care for its loved one.

A light bite on your hand, on the other hand, is a polite request to leave the animal be.

A clear sign of a cat's fighting spirit is an arched back and bristling fur.

And a raised paw with extended claws expresses dissatisfaction and aggression.

Finally, attempts from your fluffball to hug and lick you are a sign of the unconditional love it has for you.

WHY DOES MY CAT LICK ITS COAT?

Cats are very clean animals. They wash their fur several times a day, but not exclusively for purposes of hygiene. Cats also groom themselves as a way to calm down and relieve stress. If your pet is overly engaged with self-grooming, however, it can be a sign of parasites, infections, or allergies, and your veterinarian should be consulted.

More often than not, a cat will begin to groom itself after it has been punished for something. In this way, the animal is expressing either its guilt or offense. At other times, your pet may simply be grooming itself out of boredom.

THE LANGUAGE OF PURRING

There is a widely-accepted stereotype among cat owners that purring is an expression of excess feelings.

This isn't always the case, however. Purring serves different purposes for your pet:

- communication with kittens;
- an expression of comfort and contentment;
- showing the desire for something from an owner;
- thanking an owner for their care;
- comforting itself during stressful moments;
- relieving pain when injured or sick.

WHY DOES MY CAT SCREAM?

Felines may scream in the following circumstances:
- when experiencing stress or discomfort;

- when feeling pain;
- when trying to attract attention;
- when protecting territory;
- during mating.

Cats' screams are produced by an open jaw and straining vocal cords. The sound is quite unpleasant and sharp. Cats can inherently change the strength and timbre of their yells. This "cat chorus" is often performed by the animals as a mating ritual.

Cats can also make a variety of hissing and snorting sounds. Felines will hiss as a warning to an offender to back off. If at the same time, a cat arches its back and bristles its fur, it's ready to attack. Felines will often make frustrated chattering sounds when they see prey they can't reach, like birds on the other side of a window, for example.

Mother cats use the same sounds to teach their kittens to hunt. These sounds find their source at the gene level, so the cat reproduces them automatically.

THE MEANING OF "MEOW"

Despite the fact that our furry pets express their main range of emotions non-verbally, verbal communication between the pet and owner continues to exist. Cats are incredibly intelligent creatures, able to learn quickly and easily.

Living side by side with humans for so long, cats have learned from them. They too learn to use their vocal abilities to become more expressive. A meow can be affectionate, questioning, demanding, or gentle.

A meow's intonation is consistent with its purpose. Therefore, owners that are in touch with their felines can actually communicate effectively with their pets. Furthermore, these expressive cats can learn to manipulate their owners, making demands with their meows. A cat's meow is somewhat similar to the cry of a small child.

Zoopsychologists assert that cats do this intentionally in order to get what they want at any given moment. The Cornish Rex and Oriental Shorthair are among the most vocal breeds, but the top prize for talkative felines, however, rightfully goes to Siamese cats. These creatures will recite fairy tales and sing you a song. Owners of these particular talkative breeds often report bending to the will of their pets, simply for a break from the constant meowing.

COMMUNICATION OF CATS AMONGST THEMSELVES

Cats communicate with each other via their own language of smells, sounds, and body movements. The language of communication between animals is much richer and more diverse than that of humans.

The main actor in a feline's dialogue is the tail. With it, animals express their feelings, emotions, and desires:

When the tail is raised, the animal is greeting a friend or relative, but a lowered tail is an expression of discontent.

If the tail is tucked up, the cat is ready to defend its territory.

And a tail whipping from side to side is an expression of anger.

Cats that are unfamiliar with one another will freeze upon first meeting, then gradually begin to close the distance, determining whether or not they'd like to get to know one another. If they decide to say hello, they approach with their noses and sniff one another.

Cats mark their territory as a kind of bulletin board, through which they spread and read the news of their surroundings.

Communication between felines is sometimes accompanied by a form of dialogue. For example:

Cats purring with one another are friendly and calm.

A cat growling at another may be a demand to leave the first's territory.

A yowl may mark a possible attack.

And hissing will almost certainly be followed by a scuffle.

A mother cat also uses sounds to communicate with her kittens:

A low rumble may be a warning of danger.

A guttural snarl will be directed towards others when a mother cat wants them to leave her offspring.

Even cats that aren't the best of friends are usually able to coexist with one another. Cats are naturally peaceful creatures that don't like conflict or quarrels.

CULTIVATING MUTUAL UNDERSTANDING BETWEEN YOU AND YOUR CAT

To ensure no misunderstanding between owner and pet, you need to find a unique approach to fit the needs of your specific feline. First of all, follow the basic rules of respecting your cat and its space, providing it with comfortable living conditions, eliminating aggressive tendencies, never forcing it to interact with other animals against its will, and simply spending time with your fuzzy loved one to cultivate an atmosphere of care and love.

RESPECTING YOUR CAT

One of the most important elements of successful and healthy communication between you and your animal is, first and foremost, respecting the animal. Take the time to show your pet affection, but give it privacy when desired. Use a calm and gentle tone when talking to your cat.

Never squeeze your pet, disturb its sleep, pick it up when it doesn't want to be held, or forcibly grab its paws.

Another nuance of communication with your feline — let it say what it wants. Offer your cat an open palm and see how it behaves. If the animal retreats, give it time. If, on the other hand, it buries itself in your hand, show your fluffball the affection it's ready for.

Squeezing your cat and showering it with kisses is never recommended. Think how significantly large you appear to your pet. It may feel afraid or threatened at such a large creature approaching and trying to wrap the animal in its arms. Furthermore, petting your cat for too long can lead to an overabundance of sensations, scoring you a sharp bite on the hand.

There is no need to call the animal to you without good reason (petting, as far as your cat is concerned, is not a significant reason). If you abuse the attention of your whiskered friend, then it will subsequently begin to ignore your calls. An independent cat knows when to approach for affection and love.

COMFORTABLE LIVING CONDITIONS

Healthy, well-adjusted cats require comfortable living conditions. Try to view your home through the eyes of your point in order to find a compromise in cohabitation. Do not put the food bowl next to the refrigerator, or the litter box next to the washing machine. Cats are sensitive to sounds, and certain appliances might frighten them. Ensure everything the cat needs is in a quiet, private place in can go without worry.

ADMONISHING YOUR CAT

Cats become easily stressed when spoken to in a raised voice or, worse, punished physically. This will only scare and drive your pet from you, with none of the desired corrective effects. Dominating your cat will only cause it to think of you as a dangerous creature better avoided.

Furthermore, cats do not enjoy being stared at. Always use a calm voice whether scolding or praising your animal, simply adjust the timbre of your voice to match your intentions. It is best to always be consistent with your pets — do not scold and pet them at the same time, it will only lead to confusion.

Do not scold your pet by using its name. You cannot use the creature's name as an admonishment, then five minutes later call it and try to play with it or give it treats, trying to make amends. The cat will simply not understand whether it was punished or not and will carry on with the same behavior, only in your absence. When prohibiting your animal from doing something, find an alternative to their name.

SOLICITING FRIENDSHIP BETWEEN PETS

It is not your job as an owner of multiple pets to force friendship between them. In fact, you cannot do so, no matter how badly you may want to. Instead, gradually introduce your pets to one another. When bringing a new pet into the home, it is a good idea to keep them separated until they become adjusted to their new environment.

While you can't force friendship, you can do try to ease the bridge between them. You can offer a pet the other's blanket, for example, to allow them to become familiar with the new smell. If the animals do not love each other, however, you should not specifically impose any interactions between them. Over time, they will work out their own hierarchy and will be able to coexist peacefully in the same home.

STRENGTHENING YOUR RELATIONSHIP WITH YOUR PET

Your cat is a member of the family, and your mutual healthy relationship depends on effective communication. The most effective means of deepening the bond between you and your feline friend is caring for it appropriately, showing it affection, and playing games with it.

If you do not play with your pet, it will find its own forms of entertainment, often to the owner's displeasure.

It is better to find time and give the animal a little attention. Start with a daily ritual of greeting and bidding your pet farewell. Every time you leave or return home, give your cat a pet and say, "Hello" or "Goodbye."

If your cat offers its belly to be pet, it's a sign of complete trust in you. Don't ignore the offer or you risk offending your animal. In order for a cat to understand and respect its owners, it must be treated as an equal, not a creature to be subordinated. Study and learn your cat's particular expressions and moods, and you will enjoy a healthy relationship for years to come.

MY CAT IS AN ALIEN

Yes, an alien. Sometimes it really does feel like our furry friends are from another planet. These creatures can see perfectly in the dark, and at night, their eyes glow like stars.

Cats can distinguish almost all colors except red. Some are constantly talking in their cat language, similar to the babbling of a toddler. Sometimes it seems like you can even make out some words in their rambling... A Japanese company even invented a cat translation device, which, through an analysis of your pet's face and sounds, can apparently tell you exactly what kind of mood your cat is in. I, for one, could certainly use one.

Printed in Great Britain
by Amazon